# AIR VARIÉ

## Hubert Painparé

### Arranged for Clarinet and Piano by
# Paula Corley

**PIANO**

keisersouthernmusic.com

# PERFORMANCE NOTES

*Air Varie* is a theme and variations, a compositional form that originated in the Baroque period before becoming a standard form of the classical period. Edited by the International Clarinet Association's former Pedagogy Chair, Paula Corley, this delightful recital piece for clarinet and piano opens with a rubato solo for the clarinet leading to the primary theme in a slow waltz style. The first variation appears within the opening waltz section, embellishing the theme with fast, slurred passages. Variation two presents the melodic material in a slower, deliberate 4/4 meter, reminiscent of works by Carl Maria von Weber. The third and final variation recaps the theme in a fast triple meter showcasing the technical virtuosity of the performer. A closing accelerando creates a strong, exciting finish.

# Air Varie
## for Clarinet and Piano

Hubert Painpare
arranged by Paula Corley

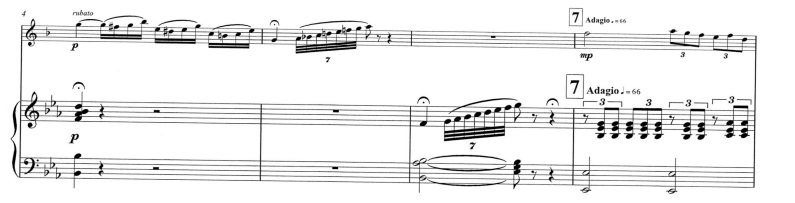

Air Varie

# Air Varie
### for Clarinet and Piano

Hubert Painpare
arranged by Paula Corley

Clarinet in B♭

Clarinet in B♭

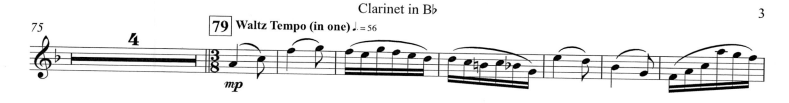

# PERFORMANCE NOTES

*Air Varie* is a theme and variations, a compositional form that originated in the Baroque period before becoming a standard form of the classical period. Edited by the International Clarinet Association's former Pedagogy Chair, Paula Corley, this delightful recital piece for clarinet and piano opens with a rubato solo for the clarinet leading to the primary theme in a slow waltz style. The first variation appears within the opening waltz section, embellishing the theme with fast, slurred passages. Variation two presents the melodic material in a slower, deliberate 4/4 meter, reminiscent of works by Carl Maria von Weber. The third and final variation recaps the theme in a fast triple meter showcasing the technical virtuosity of the performer. A closing accelerando creates a strong, exciting finish.

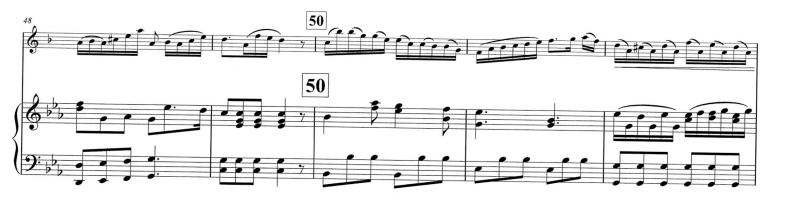

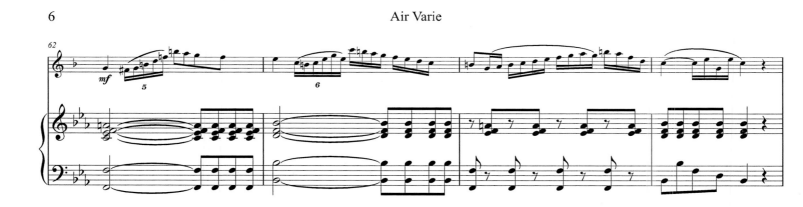

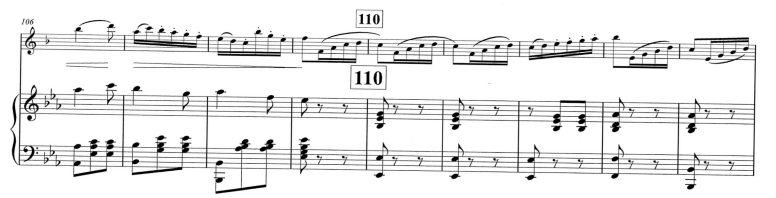

Air Varie

*Air Varie* is a theme and variations, a compositional form that originated in the Baroque period before becoming a standard form of the classical period. Edited by the International Clarinet Association's former Pedagogy Chair, Paula Corley, this delightful recital piece for clarinet and piano opens with a rubato solo for the clarinet leading to the primary theme in a slow waltz style. The first variation appears within the opening waltz section, embellishing the theme with fast, slurred passages. Variation two presents the melodic material in a slower, deliberate 4/4 meter, reminiscent of works by Carl Maria von Weber. The third and final variation recaps the theme in a fast triple meter showcasing the technical virtuosity of the performer. A closing accelerando creates a strong, exciting finish.

## ABOUT THE ARRANGER

**Paula Corley** is the Educational Advisor for Buffet Crampon North America. She has extensive teaching experience from middle school to university level, most recently as the clarinet instructor at Texas Lutheran University. While at TLU, Paula created and hosted 'clariNETWORKS' – a very popular annual event for clarinetists of all ages and band directors. Paula served as the Pedagogy Chair for the International Clarinet Association from 2018-2020 and is currently a chamber music judge for Music for All's National Chamber Music Festival. Most know her as the 'mayor' of Clarinet City, a teaching website for all ages and stages of clarinet playing.

Originally from Mississippi, Paula grew up without access to clarinet lessons, which sparked a lifelong interest in research for developing players. She is a graduate of Mississippi State University (BME) where she was named Alumnus of the Year for music in 2012-13 and Southern Methodist University (MM) where she worked with Howard Dunn. Paula taught in the Plano, Texas Independent School District for several years before moving to Asheville, NC where she served as principal clarinet in the Asheville Lyric Opera and on the faculty at Mars Hill College.

Author of *So You Want to Play the Clarinet* and *The Break* (Southern Music), Paula has performed and presented at music conferences throughout the US since 1998. She is a performing artist and clinician for Vandoren and for Buffet Crampon. Her articles have appeared in *The Clarinet*, *Vandoren WAVE*, *The Texas Bandmasters Review,* and *The Instrumentalist*. She has two commissioned works for clarinet: *Unfamiliar Territory* by Michael Markowski and *Road Trip* for clarinet quintet by Clifton Jones.

EXCLUSIVELY DISTRIBUTED BY
HAL•LEONARD®

**EAN 13**

8 40126 99058 4

*keisersouthernmusic.com*

**U.S. $9.95**

9 781638 870135

**SU841**
**HL00369423**